A.E. HOU

Poems selected by ALAN HOLLINGHURST

D0676377

A. E. HOUSMAN
Poems selected by
ALAN HOLLINGHURST

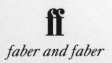

faber and faber

This selection first published in 2001
by Faber and Faber Limited
3 Queen Square London WC1N 3AU

Photoset by Parker Typesetting Service, Leicester
Printed in Italy

A CIP record for this book
is available from the British Library
ISBN 0–571–20705–7

10 9 8 7 6 5 4 3 2 1

Contents

Introduction vii

from A SHROPSHIRE LAD

    II (Loveliest of trees, the cherry now) 5
    IV Reveille 6
    VII (When smoke stood up from Ludlow) 7
    IX (On moonlit heath and lonesome bank) 8
    XI (On your midnight pallet lying) 10
    XII (When I watch the living meet) 11
    XIII (When I was one-and-twenty) 12
    XIV (There pass the careless people) 13
    XV (Look not in my eyes, for fear) 14
    XVI (It nods and curtseys and recovers) 15
    XIX To an Athlete Dying Young 16
    XXI Bredon Hill 17
    XXII (The street sounds to the soldiers' tread) 19
    XXIV (Say, lad, have you things to do?) 20
    XXVII ('Is my team ploughing?') 21
    XXVIII The Welsh Marches 23
    XXIX The Lent Lily 25
    XXX (Others, I am not the first) 26
    XXXI (On Wenlock Edge the wood's in trouble) 27
    XXXII (From far, from eve and morning) 28
    XXXV (On the idle hill of summer) 29
    XXXVI (White in the moon the long road lies) 30
    XXXVIII (The winds out of the west land blow) 31
    XL (Into my heart an air that kills) 32
    XLIV (Shot? So quick, so clean an ending?) 33
    XLVI (Bring, in this timeless grave to throw) 34
    L (*Clunton and Clunbury*) 35
    LII (Far in a western brookland) 36
    LIV (With rue my heart is laden) 37
    LXIII (I hoed and trenched and weeded) 38

from LAST POEMS

    VII (In valleys green and still) 41
    IX (The chestnut casts his flambeaux, and the
          flowers) 42
     X (Could man be drunk for ever) 43
    XV Eight O'Clock 44
    XIX (In midnights of November) 45
    XX (The night is freezing fast) 46
    XXI (The fairies break their dances) 47
  XXXIII (When the eye of day is shut) 48
  XXXVI Revolution 49
  XXXVII Epitaph on an Army of Mercenaries 50
    XL (Tell me not here, it needs not saying) 51

from MORE POEMS

    VI (I to my perils) 55
    IX (When green buds hang in the elm like dust) 56
    X (The weeping Pleiads wester) 57
  XXIII (Crossing alone the nighted ferry) 58
  XXXI (Because I liked you better) 59
  XLIII (I wake from dreams and turning) 60

from ADDITIONAL POEMS

    IX (When the bells justle in the tower) 63
  XVIII (Oh who is that young sinner with the handcuffs
          on his wrists?) 64
  XXII R.L.S. 65

Introduction

In his mid-seventies A. E. Housman described how he had written his poems: a pint of beer at lunchtime brought on a kind of sedation of the intellect, and in the course of a two- or three-hour walk afterwards, lines, and sometimes whole stanzas, of verse would flow into his mind 'with sudden and unaccountable emotion'. He regarded his poetry as a morbid secretion, like a pearl in an oyster, claiming that the irritant had generally been a period of bad health. Many of his poems retain this spontaneous quality, and effectively convey the pressures and revelations of emotional crisis; if they also seem very literary poems, little echo-chambers of poetic and biblical reference, that is doubtless because Housman was spontaneously literary too, and the resources of tradition came to him as readily and as aptly as a cry of pain. A lot of his best work has the involuntary physical effect he valued in old ballads and songs, whilst also being impeccably disciplined: the skin-shivering or tear-starting quality is secured through the formal control and metrical sixth sense of the poet. As a classical scholar, Housman remains famous for his ruthless clarity of thought, but his poems are deliberate evasions of the intellect. He saw the 'peculiar function of poetry' as being 'to transfuse emotion – not to transmit thought but to set up in the reader's sense a vibration corresponding to what was felt by the writer'.

Housman was a willing mythologist of his own work, as he was of his own psyche. His notebooks show that he worked hard at the ordering and refinement of the spontaneous fragments, and that sometimes a stanza might take decades to find its place. Though a poem such as 'Tell me not here' (*Last Poems* XL) seems naturally to be the work of an older man, there is little sense of development in Housman's poetry. *A Shropshire Lad* came out in 1896, much of it having been written in the previous year. But *Last Poems* (published in

1922, and the only other volume Housman allowed in his lifetime) contains work from the same period indistinguishable in manner from pieces written nearly thirty years later. The hauntingly dreamlike *Last Poems* VII fits a final stanza written 'long ago' to a poem of 1922; *Last Poems* IX adds a final stanza of 1922 to a poem of 1895. These were the two main periods of activity, with a sprinkling of work before and between and (very rarely) after; but the ordering of the later books, which also contain rejects from *A Shropshire Lad*, denies any importance to chronology. *More Poems* was assembled from the notebooks after Housman's death in 1936 by his brother Laurence, whose memoir *A.E.H.* contained further work included in 'Additional Poems' in the *Collected Poems* of 1939. So the final poem in this selection was written at about the same time as the first one; and its beautiful elegiac improvisation on phrases from Robert Louis Stevenson's own 'Requiem' may seem an appropriate envoy to the work of a writer who so saved and retuned his own words.

A Shropshire Lad has its memorable idiosyncrasies, its gaucheries and parodiable mannerisms, but it remains the most vital English poetry collection of the 1890s and perhaps of the whole period from the death of Tennyson until Hardy's *Satires of Circumstance* at the outbreak of the Great War. It is a fictional work, written in Highgate, secreted in walks over Hampstead Heath. Housman was a Worcestershire man, not a Salopian, though Shropshire took on romance as a largely unknown country to the west. Like many writers he was excited by an idea of a place more than by the place itself. The 'narrator' – and originally the pseudonymous author – is Terence Hearsay (a name which misleadingly suggests both Roman and Restoration comedy): very much one of the lads in his consumption of 'pints and quarts of Ludlow beer', but set apart by an almost masochistic melancholy and the habit of writing poems ('stupid stuff', according to one drinking partner). He is a figure, Housman conceded, with something of his own 'temper and view of life', though to call him a figure is perhaps a mistake. He is a presence that comes and goes, a slightly awkward convenience. Housman's own personality is too strongly felt for us to believe in Terence as a 'lad', and indeed the poems gain force from the incessant backward glances they cast from a later discontent. Housman thus appears both adolescent and old before his time, a pattern not uncommon in very repressed personalities.

Housman's avowed models were Heine (one can imagine a number of the poems as the texts of *Schwanengesang*-type Schubert songs, and they have proved richly susceptible to musical settings), the Border ballads (reflected in the grim, even melodramatic irony of some of his scenarios) and Shakespeare's songs, which strike recurrent echoes: much of the book could be seen as a set of variations on Feste's song in *Twelfth Night* ('Youth's a stuff will not endure') and *Cymbeline*'s 'Fear no more the heat o' th' sun': 'Golden lads and girls all must,/ As chimney-sweepers, come to dust.' It was the golden lads who more concerned Housman, of course; and it is perhaps the difficulty of that illicit subject which, while lending the book a fascinating tension, makes too for a certain instability of tone, clumsy humour and forced diction sometimes co-existing in a single poem with passages of limpid sensibility. It would be interesting to know to what extent readers over the past century have considered, or even acknowledged, the homosexual foundations of the book. The disguise in the conventional forms and terms of ballad, song and epigram fits so well; even if nowadays we notice, and are perhaps grateful for, its transparency, and feel that Housman was right to enlist the time-honoured dignity of these forms to his less licensed sufferings.

The poems have the effect of both expressing and concealing a great shaping crisis in Housman's life, though it is only just to say that their boldness is more remarkable than their secretiveness. In the poems' own terms Housman had 'given his heart away' and knew he would never get it back. At

Oxford he had fallen deeply and unrequitably in love with his fellow undergraduate Moses Jackson; but Jackson went to India in 1887, and subsequently married. The sense of physical and emotional separation seems to have spurred Housman into writing poetry (which he had not done since he was a boy) and into creating his metaphorical world of sundered friendship, irreversible change and exile from a scene of happiness. The book aches and sighs with loneliness, with the sleepless solitary dusks and dawns of the depressive's calendar. Amorous and sexual emotions are clouded by regret and fear; of a poem in which fear 'contends' with desire (no. xxx), Housman explained that it was about the 'unwholesome excitement of adultery', a phrase which ingeniously decoys us from the truth it voices, the impossible longing for an adulterous union with his now married friend. (Jackson died in 1923, and Housman's further burst of activity as a poet in 1922 can plausibly be put down to the emotional shock of learning of his illness. If the work seems not to develop it may be because the later crisis was in a way the same as the first crisis.)

Housman's own account of the gestation of *A Shropshire Lad* puts it down typically to a physical cause, a 'relaxed sore throat' in the first half of 1895; but it is known that he was deeply affected and agitated by the trial of Oscar Wilde, and his imprisonment at the end of May that year. Certainly the consciousness of a condemned and possibly culpable sexuality haunts the book, and though much of it was drafted before Wilde's sentencing, that event may have seemed to focus and confirm a tendency of mind in Housman himself; when he writes, 'They hang us now in Shrewsbury jail', the effect is slightly comic, but the *us* is unforgettable.

The book's early readers might well have been puzzled by its corpse-strewn landscape and wondered what massacre or epidemic had laid so many of Terence's friends low; if they're not in the pub it's because they're already in the churchyard.

A number of them have been hanged, but that only reflects the statistically abnormal proportion of murderers in Terence's social set. Housman was excited, as Kingsley Amis put it, by 'wounds imagined more than seen'; and the high mortality rate in his mythic Shropshire suggests not only a recognition of but a taste for suffering and deprivation, just as the invented fellowship of convicts and men of the soil speaks of a hunger for instinctual life in all its potential violence. An emptiness in the poet is revealed by the imaginary company he keeps; and a pathetic tension is established between Housman the young professor of Latin and his 'remembered' world which ignores or repudiates his profession, and where nothing is done but farming, drinking, courting and killing. The fantasy of rustic comradeship may be liberating, but it is also self-denying, even self-hating. In some ways it is evidently a projection of Jackson's unamenable nature and lack of common ground with Housman.

Another of the book's romances is with the soldier's life, where the courtship is with death, either for its own honour and 'cleanness' (often a suspect word in this period) or as a nihilistic reaction to spurned love – a narrative movement somewhat reminiscent of Tennyson's 'monodrama' *Maud*. If *A Shropshire Lad* has an indefinably prophetic quality, a slightly eerie and admonitory presence, it is because its preoccupations with male fellowship and lost youth were to strike so deep a chord with the generation that went to war in 1914, and with the families they left behind. Acclaim had actually been slow to come. Housman had paid for publication himself, and the book was, in the modern term, a 'sleeper'. But by the outbreak of war it was 'in every pocket'. The war drew people back to poetry, which assumed an active role as reassurance and consolation, an ordered but endless mindscape of memory and association, in which abiding values were enshrined. The numerous allusions to classic poems and the Old Testament in Housman's work must have given it a further almost subliminal resonance. Under the cover of his nostalgia, and the accuracy of his loving but unindulgent eye for flowers, trees and stars, Housman's more unorthodox persuasions and bleakly godless views (not pessimist, he insisted, merely pejorist) must also have found a thousand echoes. There can be few literary works so thronged with metaphors and euphemisms for death and the grave: the stiller town, the far dwelling, the nation that is not; the 'beautiful and death-struck' world he had drawn from his private disillusionment assumed an almost too literal universality. As Robert Lowell observed, it was as if Housman had foreseen the Somme.

Alan Hollinghurst

A. E. HOUSMAN

from A SHROPSHIRE LAD

Comhairie Chonta Átha Cliath Theas

Loveliest of trees, the cherry now
Is hung with bloom along the bough,
And stands about the woodland ride
Wearing white for Eastertide.

Now, of my threescore years and ten,
Twenty will not come again,
And take from seventy springs a score,
It only leaves me fifty more.

And since to look at things in bloom
Fifty springs are little room,
About the woodlands I will go
To see the cherry hung with snow.

Reveille

Wake: the silver dusk returning
   Up the beach of darkness brims,
And the ship of sunrise burning
   Strands upon the eastern rims.

Wake: the vaulted shadow shatters,
   Trampled to the floor it spanned,
And the tent of night in tatters
   Straws the sky-pavilioned land.

Up, lad, up, 'tis late for lying:
   Hear the drums of morning play;
Hark, the empty highways crying
   'Who'll beyond the hills away?'

Towns and countries woo together,
   Forelands beacon, belfries call;
Never lad that trod on leather
   Lived to feast his heart with all.

Up, lad: thews that lie and cumber
   Sunlit pallets never thrive;
Morns abed and daylight slumber
   Were not meant for man alive.

Clay lies still, but blood's a rover;
   Breath's a ware that will not keep.
Up, lad: when the journey's over
   There'll be time enough to sleep.

When smoke stood up from Ludlow,
    And mist blew off from Teme,
And blithe afield to ploughing
    Against the morning beam
    I strode beside my team,

The blackbird in the coppice,
    Looked out to see me stride,
And hearkened as I whistled
    The trampling team beside,
    And fluted and replied:

'Lie down, lie down, young yeoman;
    What use to rise and rise?
Rise man a thousand mornings
    Yet down at last he lies,
    And then the man is wise.'

I heard the tune he sang me,
    And spied his yellow bill;
I picked a stone and aimed it
    And threw it with a will:
    Then the bird was still.

Then my soul within me
    Took up the blackbird's strain,
And still beside the horses
    Along the dewy lane
    It sang the song again:

'Lie down, lie down, young yeoman;
    The sun moves always west;
The road one treads to labour
    Will lead one home to rest,
    And that will be the best.'

On moonlit heath and lonesome bank
    The sheep beside me graze;
And yon the gallows used to clank
    Fast by the four cross ways.

A careless shepherd once would keep
    The flocks by moonlight there,*
And high amongst the glimmering sheep
    The dead man stood on air.

They hang us now in Shrewsbury jail:
    The whistles blow forlorn,
And trains all night groan on the rail
    To men that die at morn.

There sleeps in Shrewsbury jail to-night,
    Or wakes, as may betide,
A better lad, if things went right,
    Than most that sleep outside.

And naked to the hangman's noose
    The morning clocks will ring
A neck God made for other use
    Than strangling in a string.

And sharp the link of life will snap,
    And dead on air will stand
Heels that held up as straight a chap
    As treads upon the land.

So here I'll watch the night and wait
    To see the morning shine,
When he will hear the stroke of eight
    And not the stroke of nine;

* Hanging in chains was called keeping sheep by moonlight.

And wish my friends as sound a sleep
    As lads' I did not know,
That shepherded the moonlit sheep
    A hundred years ago.

On your midnight pallet lying,
    Listen, and undo the door:
Lads that waste the light in sighing
    In the dark should sigh no more;
Night should ease a lover's sorrow;
Therefore, since I go to-morrow,
    Pity me before.

In the land to which I travel,
    The far dwelling, let me say —
Once, if here the couch is gravel,
    In a kinder bed I lay,
And the breast the darnel smothers
Rested once upon another's
    When it was not clay.

XII

When I watch the living meet,
    And the moving pageant file
Warm and breathing through the street
    Where I lodge a little while,

If the heats of hate and lust
    In the house of flesh are strong,
Let me mind the house of dust
    Where my sojourn shall be long.

In the nation that is not
    Nothing stands that stood before;
There revenges are forgot,
    And the hater hates no more;

Lovers lying two and two
    Ask not whom they sleep beside,
And the bridegroom all night through
    Never turns him to the bride.

When I was one-and-twenty
  I heard a wise man say,
'Give crowns and pounds and guineas
  But not your heart away;
Give pearls away and rubies
  But keep your fancy free.'
But I was one-and-twenty,
  No use to talk to me.

When I was one-and-twenty
  I heard him say again,
'The heart out of the bosom
  Was never given in vain;
'Tis paid with sighs a plenty
  And sold for endless rue.'
And I am two-and-twenty,
  And oh, 'tis true, 'tis true.

XIV

There pass the careless people
    That call their souls their own:
Here by the road I loiter,
    How idle and alone.

Ah, past the plunge of plummet,
    In seas I cannot sound,
My heart and soul and senses,
    World without end, are drowned.

His folly has not fellow
    Beneath the blue of day
That gives to man or woman
    His heart and soul away.

There flowers no balm to sain him
    From east of earth to west
That's lost for everlasting
    The heart out of his breast.

Here by the labouring highway
    With empty hands I stroll:
Sea-deep, till doomsday morning,
    Lie lost my heart and soul.

Look not in my eyes, for fear
    They mirror true the sight I see,
And there you find your face too clear
    And love it and be lost like me.
One the long nights through must lie
    Spent in star-defeated sighs,
But why should you as well as I
    Perish? gaze not in my eyes.

A Grecian lad, as I hear tell,
    One that many loved in vain,
Looked into a forest well
    And never looked away again.
There, when the turf in springtime flowers,
    With downward eye and gazes sad,
Stands amid the glancing showers
    A jonquil, not a Grecian lad.

XVI

It nods and curtseys and recovers
   When the wind blows above,
The nettle on the graves of lovers
   That hanged themselves for love.

The nettle nods, the wind blows over,
   The man, he does not move,
The lover of the grave, the lover
   That hanged himself for love.

To an Athlete Dying Young

The time you won your town the race
We chaired you through the market-place;
Man and boy stood cheering by,
And home we brought you shoulder-high.

To-day, the road all runners come,
Shoulder-high we bring you home,
And set you at your threshold down,
Townsman of a stiller town.

Smart lad, to slip betimes away
From fields where glory does not stay
And early though the laurel grows
It withers quicker than the rose.

Eyes the shady night has shut
Cannot see the record cut,
And silence sounds no worse than cheers
After earth has stopped the ears:

Now you will not swell the rout
Of lads that wore their honours out,
Runners whom renown outran
And the name died before the man.

So set, before its echoes fade,
The fleet foot on the sill of shade,
And hold to the low lintel up
The still-defended challenge-cup.

And round that early-laurelled head
Will flock to gaze the strengthless dead,
And find unwithered on its curls
The garland briefer than a girl's.

Bredon* Hill

In summertime on Bredon
   The bells they sound so clear;
Round both the shires they ring them
   In steeples far and near,
   A happy noise to hear.

Here of a Sunday morning
   My love and I would lie,
And see the coloured counties,
   And hear the larks so high
   About us in the sky.

The bells would ring to call her
   In valleys miles away:
'Come all to church, good people;
   Good people, come and pray.'
   But here my love would stay.

And I would turn and answer
   Among the springing thyme,
'Oh, peal upon our wedding,
   And we will hear the chime,
   And come to church in time.'

But when the snows at Christmas
   On Bredon top were strown,
My love rose up so early
   And stole out unbeknown
   And went to church alone.

They tolled the one bell only,
   Groom there was none to see,
The mourners followed after,
   And so to church went she,
   And would not wait for me.

* Pronounced Breedon.

The bells they sound on Bredon,
    And still the steeples hum.
'Come all to church, good people,' –
    Oh, noisy bells, be dumb;
    I hear you, I will come.

The street sounds to the soldiers' tread,
    And out we troop to see:
A single redcoat turns his head,
    He turns and looks at me.

My man, from sky to sky's so far,
    We never crossed before;
Such leagues apart the world's ends are,
    We're like to meet no more;

What thoughts at heart have you and I
    We cannot stop to tell;
But dead or living, drunk or dry,
    Soldier, I wish you well.

Say, lad, have you things to do?
　　Quick then, while your day's at prime.
Quick, and if 'tis work for two,
　　Here am I, man: now's your time.

Send me now, and I shall go;
　　Call me, I shall hear you call;
Use me ere they lay me low
　　Where a man's no use at all;

Ere the wholesome flesh decay,
　　And the willing nerve be numb,
And the lips lack breath to say,
　　'No, my lad, I cannot come.'

'Is my team ploughing,
    That I was used to drive
And hear the harness jingle
    When I was man alive?'

Ay, the horses trample,
    The harness jingles now;
No change though you lie under
    The land you used to plough.

'Is football playing
    Along the river shore,
With lads to chase the leather,
    Now I stand up no more?'

Ay, the ball is flying,
    The lads play heart and soul;
The goal stands up, the keeper
    Stands up to keep the goal.

'Is my girl happy,
    That I thought hard to leave,
And has she tired of weeping
    As she lies down at eve?'

Ay, she lies down lightly,
    She lies not down to weep:
Your girl is well contented.
    Be still, my lad, and sleep.

'Is my friend hearty,
    Now I am thin and pine,
And has he found to sleep in
    A better bed than mine?'

21

Yes, lad, I lie easy,
    I lie as lads would choose;
I cheer a dead man's sweetheart,
    Never ask me whose.

The Welsh Marches

High the vanes of Shrewsbury gleam
Islanded in Severn stream;
The bridges from the steepled crest
Cross the water east and west.

The flag of morn in conqueror's state
Enters at the English gate:
The vanquished eve, as night prevails,
Bleeds upon the road to Wales.

Ages since the vanquished bled
Round my mother's marriage-bed;
There the ravens feasted far
About the open house of war:

When Severn down to Buildwas ran
Coloured with the death of man,
Couched upon her brother's grave
The Saxon got me on the slave.

The sound of fight is silent long
That began the ancient wrong;
Long the voice of tears is still
That wept of old the endless ill.

In my heart it has not died,
The war that sleeps on Severn side;
They cease not fighting, east and west,
On the marches of my breast.

Here the truceless armies yet
Trample, rolled in blood and sweat;
They kill and kill and never die;
And I think that each is I.

None will part us, none undo
The knot that makes one flesh of two,
Sick with hatred, sick with pain,
Strangling – When shall we be slain?

When shall I be dead and rid
Of the wrong my father did?
How long, how long, till spade and hearse
Put to sleep my mother's curse?

XXIX
The Lent Lily

'Tis spring; come out to ramble
  The hilly brakes around,
For under thorn and bramble
  About the hollow ground
  The primroses are found.

And there's the windflower chilly
  With all the winds at play,
And there's the Lenten lily
  That has not long to stay
  And dies on Easter day.

And since till girls go maying
  You find the primrose still,
And find the windflower playing
  With every wind at will,
  But not the daffodil,

Bring baskets now, and sally
  Upon the spring's array,
And bear from hill and valley
  The daffodil away
  That dies on Easter day.

XXX

Others, I am not the first,
Have willed more mischief than they durst:
If in the breathless night I too
Shiver now, 'tis nothing new.

More than I, if truth were told,
Have stood and sweated hot and cold,
And through their reins in ice and fire
Fear contended with desire.

Agued once like me were they,
But I like them shall win my way
Lastly to the bed of mould
Where there's neither heat nor cold.

But from my grave across my brow
Plays no wind of healing now,
And fire and ice within me fight
Beneath the suffocating night.

On Wenlock Edge the wood's in trouble;
   His forest fleece the Wrekin heaves;
The gale, it plies the saplings double,
   And thick on Severn snow the leaves.

'Twould blow like this through holt and hanger
   When Uricon the city stood:
'Tis the old wind in the old anger,
   But then it threshed another wood.

Then, 'twas before my time, the Roman
   At yonder heaving hill would stare:
The blood that warms an English yeoman,
   The thoughts that hurt him, they were there.

There, like the wind through woods in riot,
   Through him the gale of life blew high;
The tree of man was never quiet:
   Then 'twas the Roman, now 'tis I.

The gale, it plies the saplings double,
   It blows so hard, 'twill soon be gone:
To-day the Roman and his trouble
   Are ashes under Uricon.

From far, from eve and morning
   And yon twelve-winded sky,
The stuff of life to knit me
   Blew hither: here am I.

Now – for a breath I tarry
   Nor yet disperse apart –
Take my hand quick and tell me,
   What have you in your heart.

Speak now, and I will answer;
   How shall I help you, say;
Ere to the wind's twelve quarters
   I take my endless way.

XXXV

On the idle hill of summer,
    Sleepy with the flow of streams,
Far I hear the steady drummer
    Drumming like a noise in dreams.

Far and near and low and louder
    On the roads of earth go by,
Dear to friends and food for powder,
    Soldiers marching, all to die.

East and west on fields forgotten
    Bleach the bones of comrades slain,
Lovely lads and dead and rotten;
    None that go return again.

Far the calling bugles hollo,
    High the screaming fife replies,
Gay the files of scarlet follow:
    Woman bore me, I will rise.

White in the moon the long road lies,
    The moon stands blank above;
White in the moon the long road lies
    That leads me from my love.

Still hangs the hedge without a gust,
    Still, still the shadows stay:
My feet upon the moonlit dust
    Pursue the ceaseless way.

The world is round, so travellers tell,
    And straight though reach the track,
Trudge on, trudge on, 'twill all be well,
    The way will guide one back.

But ere the circle homeward hies
    Far, far must it remove:
White in the moon the long road lies
    That leads me from my love.

XXXVIII

The winds out of the west land blow,
  My friends have breathed them there;
Warm with the blood of lads I know
  Comes east the sighing air.

It fanned their temples, filled their lungs,
  Scattered their forelocks free;
My friends made words of it with tongues
  That talk no more to me.

Their voices, dying as they fly,
  Loose on the wind are sown;
The names of men blow soundless by,
  My fellows' and my own.

Oh lads, at home I heard you plain,
  But here your speech is still,
And down the sighing wind in vain
  You hollo from the hill.

The wind and I, we both were there,
  But neither long abode;
Now through the friendless world we fare
  And sigh upon the road.

Into my heart an air that kills
   From yon far country blows:
What are those blue remembered hills,
   What spires, what farms are those?

That is the land of lost content,
   I see it shining plain,
The happy highways where I went
   And cannot come again.

Shot? So quick, so clean an ending?
  Oh that was right, lad, that was brave:
Yours was not an ill for mending,
  'Twas best to take it to the grave.

Oh you had forethought, you could reason,
  And saw your road and where it led,
And early wise and brave in season
  Put the pistol to your head.

Oh soon, and better so than later
  After long disgrace and scorn,
You shot dead the household traitor,
  The soul that should not have been born.

Right you guessed the rising morrow
  And scorned to tread the mire you must:
Dust's your wages, son of sorrow,
  But men may come to worse than dust.

Souls undone, undoing others, –
  Long time since the tale began.
You would not live to wrong your brothers:
  Oh lad, you died as fits a man.

Now to your grave shall friend and stranger
  With ruth and some with envy come:
Undishonoured, clear of danger,
  Clean of guilt, pass hence and home.

Turn safe to rest, no dreams, no waking;
  And here, man, here's the wreath I've made:
'Tis not a gift that's worth the taking,
  But wear it and it will not fade.

Bring, in this timeless grave to throw,
No cypress, sombre on the snow;
Snap not from the bitter yew
His leaves that live December through;
Break no rosemary, bright with rime
And sparkling to the cruel clime;
Nor plod the winter land to look
For willows in the icy brook
To cast them leafless round him: bring
No spray that ever buds in spring.

But if the Christmas field has kept
Awns the last gleaner overstept,
Or shrivelled flax, whose flower is blue
A single season, never two;
Or if one haulm whose year is o'er
Shivers on the upland frore,
– Oh, bring from hill and stream and plain
Whatever will not flower again,
To give him comfort: he and those
Shall bide eternal bedfellows
Where low upon the couch he lies
Whence he never shall arise.

Clunton and Clunbury,
  Clungunford and Clun,
Are the quietest places
  Under the sun.

In valleys of springs of rivers,
  By Ony and Teme and Clun,
The country for easy livers,
  The quietest under the sun,

We still had sorrows to lighten,
  One could not be always glad,
And lads knew trouble at Knighton
  When I was a Knighton lad.

By bridges that Thames runs under,
  In London, the town built ill,
'Tis sure small matter for wonder
  If sorrow is with one still.

And if as a lad grows older
  The troubles he bears are more,
He carries his griefs on a shoulder
  That handselled them long before.

Where shall one halt to deliver
  This luggage I'd lief set down?
Not Thames, not Teme is the river,
  Nor London nor Knighton the town:

'Tis a long way further than Knighton,
  A quieter place than Clun,
Where doomsday may thunder and lighten
  And little 'twill matter to one.

Far in a western brookland
   That bred me long ago
The poplars stand and tremble
   By pools I used to know.

There, in the windless night-time,
   The wanderer, marvelling why,
Halts on the bridge to hearken
   How soft the poplars sigh.

He hears: no more remembered
   In fields where I was known,
Here I lie down in London
   And turn to rest alone.

There, by the starlit fences,
   The wanderer halts and hears
My soul that lingers sighing
   About the glimmering weirs.

With rue my heart is laden
    For golden friends I had,
For many a rose-lipt maiden
    And many a lightfoot lad.

By brooks too broad for leaping
    The lightfoot boys are laid;
The rose-lipt girls are sleeping
    In fields where roses fade.

I hoed and trenched and weeded,
    And took the flowers to fair:
I brought them home unheeded;
    The hue was not the wear.

So up and down I sow them
    For lads like me to find,
When I shall lie below them,
    A dead man out of mind.

Some seed the birds devour,
    And some the season mars,
But here and there will flower
    The solitary stars,

And fields will yearly bear them
    As light-leaved spring comes on,
And luckless lads will wear them
    When I am dead and gone.

from LAST POEMS

VII

In valleys green and still
    Where lovers wander maying
They hear from over hill
    A music playing.

Behind the drum and fife,
    Past hawthornwood and hollow,
Through earth and out of life
    The soldiers follow.

The soldier's is the trade:
    In any wind or weather
He steals the heart of maid
    And man together.

The lover and his lass
    Beneath the hawthorn lying
Have heard the soldiers pass,
    And both are sighing.

And down the distance they
    With dying note and swelling
Walk the resounding way
    To the still dwelling.

IX

The chestnut casts his flambeaux, and the flowers
    Stream from the hawthorn on the wind away,
The doors clap to, the pane is blind with showers.
    Pass me the can, lad; there's an end of May.

There's one spoilt spring to scant our mortal lot,
    One season ruined of our little store.
May will be fine next year as like as not:
    Oh ay, but then we shall be twenty-four.

We for a certainty are not the first
    Have sat in taverns while the tempest hurled
Their hopeful plans to emptiness, and cursed
    Whatever brute and blackguard made the world.

It is in truth iniquity on high
    To cheat our sentenced souls of aught they crave,
And mar the merriment as you and I
    Fare on our long fool's-errand to the grave.

Iniquity it is; but pass the can.
    My lad, no pair of kings our mothers bore;
Our only portion is the estate of man:
    We want the moon, but we shall get no more.

If here to-day the cloud of thunder lours
    To-morrow it will hie on far behests;
The flesh will grieve on other bones than ours
    Soon, and the soul will mourn in other breasts.

The troubles of our proud and angry dust
    Are from eternity, and shall not fail.
Bear them we can, and if we can we must.
    Shoulder the sky, my lad, and drink your ale.

X

Could man be drunk for ever
  With liquor, love, or fights,
Lief should I rouse at morning
  And lief lie down of nights.

But men at whiles are sober
  And think by fits and starts,
And if they think, they fasten
  Their hands upon their hearts.

XV
Eight O'Clock

He stood, and heard the steeple
    Sprinkle the quarters on the morning town.
One, two, three, four, to market-place and people
    It tossed them down.

Strapped, noosed, nighing his hour,
    He stood and counted them and cursed his luck;
And then the clock collected in the tower
    Its strength, and struck.

In midnights of November,
    When Dead Man's Fair is nigh,
And danger in the valley,
    And anger in the sky,

Around the huddling homesteads
    The leafless timber roars,
And the dead call the dying
    And finger at the doors.

Oh, yonder faltering fingers
    Are hands I used to hold;
Their false companion drowses
    And leaves them in the cold.

Oh, to the bed of ocean,
    To Africk and to Ind,
I will arise and follow
    Along the rainy wind.

The night goes out and under
    With all its train forlorn;
Hues in the east assemble
    And cocks crow up the morn.

The living are the living
    And dead the dead will stay,
And I will sort with comrades
    That face the beam of day.

The night is freezing fast,
  To-morrow comes December;
    And winterfalls of old
Are with me from the past;
  And chiefly I remember
    How Dick would hate the cold.

Fall, winter, fall; for he,
  Prompt hand and headpiece clever,
    Has woven a winter robe,
And made of earth and sea
  His overcoat for ever,
    And wears the turning globe.

XXI

The fairies break their dances
  And leave the printed lawn,
And up from India glances
  The silver sail of dawn.

The candles burn their sockets,
  The blinds let through the day,
The young man feels his pockets
  And wonders what's to pay.

XXXIII

When the eye of day is shut,
   And the stars deny their beams,
And about the forest hut
   Blows the roaring wood of dreams,

From deep clay, from desert rock,
   From the sunk sands of the main,
Come not at my door to knock,
   Hearts that loved me not again.

Sleep, be still, turn to your rest
   In the lands where you are laid;
In far lodgings east and west
   Lie down on the beds you made.

In gross marl, in blowing dust,
   In the drowned ooze of the sea,
Where you would not, lie you must,
   Lie you must, and not with me.

XXXVI
Revolution

West and away the wheels of darkness roll,
   Day's beamy banner up the east is borne,
Spectres and fears, the nightmare and her foal,
   Drown in the golden deluge of the morn.

But over sea and continent from sight
   Safe to the Indies has the earth conveyed
The vast and moon-eclipsing cone of night,
   Her towering foolscap of eternal shade.

See, in mid heaven the sun is mounted; hark,
   The belfries tingle to the noonday chime.
'Tis silent, and the subterranean dark
   Has crossed the nadir, and begins to climb.

Epitaph on an Army of Mercenaries

These, in the day when heaven was falling,
    The hour when earth's foundations fled,
Followed their mercenary calling
    And took their wages and are dead.

Their shoulders held the sky suspended;
    They stood, and earth's foundations stay;
What God abandoned, these defended,
    And saved the sum of things for pay.

Tell me not here, it needs not saying,
  What tune the enchantress plays
In aftermaths of soft September
  Or under blanching mays,
For she and I were long acquainted
  And I knew all her ways.

On russet floors, by waters idle,
  The pine lets fall its cone;
The cuckoo shouts all day at nothing
  In leafy dells alone;
And traveller's joy beguiles in autumn
  Hearts that have lost their own.

On acres of the seeded grasses
  The changing burnish heaves;
Or marshalled under moons of harvest
  Stand still all night the sheaves;
Or beeches strip in storms for winter
  And stain the wind with leaves.

Possess, as I possessed a season,
  The countries I resign,
Where over elmy plains the highway
  Would mount the hills and shine,
And full of shade the pillared forest
  Would murmur and be mine.

For nature, heartless, witless nature,
  Will neither care nor know
What stranger's feet may find the meadow
  And trespass there and go,
Nor ask amid the dews of morning
  If they are mine or no.

from MORE POEMS

I to my perils
   Of cheat and charmer
   Came clad in armour
     By stars benign.
Hope lies to mortals
   And most believe her,
   But man's deceiver
     Was never mine.

The thoughts of others
   Were light and fleeting,
   Of lovers' meeting
     Or luck or fame.
Mine were of trouble,
   And mine were steady,
   So I was ready
     When trouble came.

IX

When green buds hang in the elm like dust
   And sprinkle the lime like rain,
Forth I wander, forth I must,
   And drink of life again.
Forth I must by hedgerow bowers
   To look at the leaves uncurled,
And stand in the fields where cuckoo-flowers
   Are lying about the world.

X

The weeping Pleiads wester,
  And the moon is under seas;
From bourn to bourn of midnight
  Far sighs the rainy breeze:

It sighs from a lost country
  To a land I have not known;
The weeping Pleiads wester,
  And I lie down alone.

XXIII

Crossing alone the nighted ferry
  With the one coin for fee,
Whom, on the wharf of Lethe waiting,
  Count you to find? Not me.

The brisk fond lackey to fetch and carry,
  The true, sick-hearted slave,
Expect him not in the just city
  And free land of the grave.

Because I liked you better
   Than suits a man to say,
It irked you, and I promised
   To throw the thought away.

To put the world between us
   We parted, stiff and dry;
'Good-bye,' said you, 'forget me.'
   'I will, no fear,' said I.

If here, where clover whitens
   The dead man's knoll, you pass,
And no tall flower to meet you
   Starts in the trefoiled grass,

Halt by the headstone naming
   The heart no longer stirred,
And say the lad that loved you
   Was one that kept his word.

XLIII

I wake from dreams and turning
　My vision on the height
I scan the beacons burning
　About the fields of night.

Each in its steadfast station
　Inflaming heaven they flare;
They sign with conflagration
　The empty moors of air.

The signal-fires of warning
　They blaze, but none regard;
And on through night to morning
　The world runs ruinward.

from ADDITIONAL POEMS

IX

When the bells justle in the tower
   The hollow night amid,
Then on my tongue the taste is sour
   Of all I ever did.

Oh who is that young sinner with the handcuffs on his
    wrists?
And what has he been after that they groan and shake their
    fists?
And wherefore is he wearing such a conscience-stricken air?
Oh they're taking him to prison for the colour of his hair.

'Tis a shame to human nature, such a head of hair as his;
In the good old time 'twas hanging for the colour that it is;
Though hanging isn't bad enough and flaying would be fair
For the nameless and abominable colour of his hair.

Oh a deal of pains he's taken and a pretty price he's paid
To hide his poll or dye it of a mentionable shade;
But they've pulled the beggar's hat off for the world to see
    and stare,
And they're haling him to justice for the colour of his hair.

Now 'tis oakum for his fingers and the treadmill for his feet
And the quarry-gang on Portland in the cold and in the heat,
And between his spells of labour in the time he has to spare
He can curse the God that made him for the colour of his
    hair.

XXII
R.L.S.

Home is the sailor, home from sea:
   Her far-borne canvas furled
The ship pours shining on the quay
   The plunder of the world.

Home is the hunter from the hill:
   Fast in the boundless snare
All flesh lies taken at his will
   And every fowl of air.

'Tis evening on the moorland free,
   The starlit wave is still:
Home is the sailor from the sea,
   The hunter from the hill.